TODD BYRD

From Prison to Pulpit

TODD BYRD

From Prison to Pulpit

Todd Byrd
As Told to Sherry Anderson

Table of Contents

Foreword

❧

I was first introduced to Todd Byrd and his incredible story through a mutual friend. Of course, like most people who are excited about someone, she couldn't contain her enthusiasm for what God was doing through this young man. She fed me tidbits of a story that only later would I fully appreciate, once I had immersed myself into Todd's life and ministry.

As you will discover in the pages of this book, Todd's early years were marred with hardship, tragedy, and rebellion. His story is as compelling as it is heartbreaking at times. I found myself immediately identifying with this troubled young man, but not in the ways you might think. Having spent the last twenty-nine years of my life as a police officer, I've met a hundred Todd Byrds, maybe more. That is, pre-Christ Todd Byrds. Young men (and women) who are trapped in the downward spiral of abuse, drug and alcohol addiction, and the vicious cycles of crime and violence. Brokenness is more the rule in the world than the exception, at least from my slightly skewed law enforcement point of view.

Todd's story is different, though. Remarkably different. God's transformative power is so wonderfully displayed in Todd's journey to faith and beyond that even the most cynical person will be compelled to read on. The Lord has given Todd hope where there was only helplessness before, peace where turmoil once reigned. Once a prisoner, now a pastor, Todd's amazing life personifies the Gospel.

A wise deputy once told me that whenever he had a new trainee, he would ask them a simple question: "In God's sight and in God's judgement, what's the only thing that separates the guy in the cage in backseat from us?"

Usually, the trainee would have no idea how to respond. The deputy would then knock on the divider and say, "Only this plexiglass. We're all the same in God's sight. Sinners desperately in need of a Savior."

Todd reminds us of that. Whether you are a criminal and prisoner or a career cop or homemaker, the Gospel and God's grace is the same for everyone—and available to everyone. We are all in need of the Savior, and Todd's story and his ministry have impacted countless people, including me, for the cause of Christ. I hope and pray as you read this book that you will open your mind and your heart to not just Todd's story, but what could be your story as you let God take hold of your life.

Mark Mynheir
Author and former homicide detective whose law enforcement career also included serving as an undercover narcotics agent and a S.W.A.T. team member.

Acknowledgements

❦

I want to thank God for sending His Son, so I could be redeemed! I want to thank my beautiful wife, Dee Byrd, for standing by my side. I love you! I want say a big thanks to Sam and Tracey Gregory, Larry Eddings, Steve Patterson, Chris Smith, Stan Nunley, Chris Carter, Judge Bonds and Ms. Patsy from Milan Drug Court, and so many more. Thank all of you for seeing in me what I could not see in myself. Thank you, Sherry Anderson, for your love of our Father. It pours out in everything you do. Thank you for letting me tell you my life story, and for your willingness to write it. You are a great godly woman, and it's been an honor to work with you.

Chapter 1
Chaos

I stepped over to the window, looked out, and saw a sea of blue lights flashing wildly. The police were everywhere. I remembered an old, worthless gun we had in a closet. I grabbed it and ran out on the back porch. I frantically pointed the gun in all directions at the police. I was afraid they'd come to kill me.

My parents, hiding behind our camper in the driveway, screamed to the police. "Don't shoot! Don't shoot! That gun doesn't have a trigger!"

A policeman shouted at me, "Get on the ground!"

I hollered back, "*You* get on the ground!"

Some officers rushed me, and I hit the ground with a thud, driven into the dirt. I was terrified. They tied me up and put me in a police car, then went straight to the Emergency Room. Once there, I came out of the stupor for a minute at a time. I saw Dad crying. I'd never seen him cry in my whole life.

A foreign doctor came in. He asked me, "What drugs have you taken?"

I said, "None."

He patted me on the shoulder and said, "You are going to be okay." Then he winked at me. When he did that, I snapped.

"Ain't no man supposed to wink at another man!" I grabbed him by the throat, and the deputies right outside the room rushed in and pulled me off him. While they held me down, he jabbed me with a shot needle. My body began to relax, and they put me into the police car. I saw where they were headed down the road and realized they were taking me out of the county. They weren't supposed to do that. I was terrified. I just *knew* they were going to kill me.

***

The night had begun with our usual partying. We used anything available to get high. I had accidently taken an overdose of LSD and also a pod that grows wild called gypsum seed (Jimson weed). Plant parts can be brewed as a tea or chewed, and seed pods can be eaten. We took two pods and removed the seeds and put a bunch of them in a two-liter Dr. Pepper. Normally people only put two seeds in, but we put them *all* in. So we had us some Dr. Pepper and before long, started seeing things and talking crazy. It scared us.

After a while, I went outside and walked through the woods toward my house. When I got there, paranoid and hallucinating, I thought my parents and brother were the police. I rushed into my bedroom and locked the door. It got real quiet. I cracked open the bedroom door and looked out through the narrow space. They were gone. I had gone to the window, and that's when I had seen all the blue lights outside.

So, now in a haze, I rode in the back of the police car and in my paranoia, just *knew* they were going to kill me. Instead, we arrived at the State Psychiatric Hospital in Bolivar, Tennessee. I was admitted with a "Request for Immediate Examination for Emergency Admission." They put me in the substance abuse ward under a suicide watch. The admittance was for 60 days.

When the lady booked me into the hospital, she said, "Everything here is confidential. You don't have to use your real name. You can pick another name, like Bob or John."

I said, "I am not a snitch. My name is Todd David Byrd. Put that on my nametag. I noticed later that all the other patients had only a first name on their tag and mine said, "Todd David Byrd."

They gave me medication, and as I settled down I realized I was surrounded by people in there who had gone crazy from doing drugs. I hadn't slept for four days before I arrived and was awake four more before being able to sleep.

After I had been there a few days, I was walking in my unit. There was an older black gentlemen dressed in Army fatigues. As we walked by each other, he deliberately bumped into me.

I said, "*Excuse you.*"

He sneered and bared his teeth aggressively. A little later, he bumped into me again. I pointed my finger at him and said, "You bump me again and I am going to bust your head!" I was 18 years old and knew I was strong. I wasn't afraid of anything. He just looked at me crazy, but didn't bump me again that day.

Four patients stayed in each unit. That night I went to bed and, for the first time in days, slept through the night. I woke up the next morning, opened a drawer in the dresser by my bed, and pulled out a pair of socks. As I pulled them on, my foot went all the way through the sock and out the toe. I grabbed another pair and the same thing happened. Every pair of my socks had the toe section cut off. I walked barefoot into the day room, and there sat the man in Army fatigues with a headband that *matched* my socks. He stared at me and, without uttering a word, his cold eyes said, "I *could* have killed you in your sleep." This guy had stood over me while I slept and must have used a razor blade to cut out the toes of my socks. He had stitched them together and tied a band around his head like Rambo. I was scared to death! TV monitors surveyed our movements around the clock, and yet this guy came into my room and did this. Scared, I called my mom and said, "Get me outta here!"

She couldn't do anything. I had to ride out the full 60 days. The Rambo episode was on the fifth day. Believe me, after that, I minded my own business and left that guy alone.

Every morning, someone on staff asked me, "Do you feel like killing yourself today?"

I said, "No, I *never* felt like killing myself."

Finally, at the end of the 60 days, the doctor asked that question again.

I said, "No. I feel like killing *you*."

He laughed and said to the nurse, "He's ready to go home."

Chapter 2
Choosing the Wrong Track

I started smoking marijuana and drinking alcohol when my brother Keith introduced me to it at twelve years old. By the age of 14, I had progressed to heavier drugs. He said it would give me energy if I did meth before playing football. He had a connection with a gang to get the drugs, so they were available whenever I wanted them.

The school bus picked me up out in the country every day. After arriving at the campus, I walked to the back of the parking lot. The "cooler" kids parked back there and hung out by their cars. We were allowed to smoke cigarettes if we brought a permission slip from our parents. So I went back there and hung out with the smokers – only my group was smoking pot during the 20 minutes before the first bell rang.

After lunch, we hung out by the vocation building, smoking weed and getting high. I usually slept through Study Hall. At 2:00 PM, we had P.E. One day my defensive coach asked me, "What is that smell? I smell a strong odor from you. Why are your eyes so red?"

"It's allergies," I said.

There was no hiding what my eyes looked like. Smoking pot dilates blood vessels and capillaries, and my bloodshot eyes told on me. I concocted a lie to cover for it. My line to those who mentioned it became, "I've got real bad allergies." I had prepared my lies so well that my parents took me to the doctor, and he confirmed that I had allergies. So I would tell them whenever there was a comment or question about my eyes, "It's allergies. Ask my mom. You can call her." Or I said, "Do I need a doctor's note?" I repeated this day after day. I thought everybody around me was blind to what was going on since my lie covered it up.

During football season, we stayed after school for practice. One day the coach came to me and he said, "You smell just like pot. And man, your eyes are red."

I said, "Well, you know I got allergies."

Coach said, "Todd, today we are going to see how bad them allergies are!"

He could see right through my lies. He knew the lifestyle I was living.

He said, "We're going to the school office and, like I said, we are going to see how bad them allergies are."

When we got there, he had me sit in the waiting room. Several people came in and made comments.

"Whew! What's that smell?"

Another said, "Man, I smell marijuana!"

That got me steadily becoming more nervous about the situation. The secretary called me into the office, and Coach Tucker said, "You know this year they passed a law. You're playing football and when you signed up, you and your parents signed an agreement for a random drug test. The Milan Police Department is on the way to escort you to the Emergency Room, and you are going to be giving a urine sample."

My mind whirled. I decided to tell them someone put something in my drink. I thought, *There has got to be some way out of this.*

The police arrived and escorted me to my first ride in a police car. They drove to the E.R. at Milan General Hospital. I got in there and thought, *Uh-oh I'm not going to lie my way out of this one. I'm in trouble.*

I looked at the nurse as she shut the door.

"Sir, you need to take this cup, go in that bathroom, and give me a urine sample."

I said, "Can you do it for me?"

She said, with a cold look, "I most certainly will not!"

I thought, *I got a "square" doctor and I'm in trouble.*

She said, "Young man, you go in that bathroom and give me a sample."

Well, I didn't have any experience and didn't know any better. I went in there and scooped water out of the commode and came out and set it down. "There you go."

After a moment, she said, "We've got a problem. First of all, it doesn't register on the temperature gauge and second of all, are you a Smurf?" She pointed to the blue water in my cup.

"Well, uhh…well." I went back in there and urinated in a new cup.

She said, "We're going to send this off, and in three weeks the results will come back."

I went out and got in the car with my mom. She said, "We're going to show them."

I said, "Yes ma'am." She was sure that it was a

mistake and I only had allergies. I knew I was just buying time and continued in my classes as usual.

The three weeks went by, then someone in the school office called and asked Mama to come in. When she got there, they got me out of class. The head coach was also the principal of the school, and he had us sit in chairs across the desk from him. In his hand he held an envelope. He pulled out the folded document and said, "Todd has tested positive for marijuana and methamphetamine."

Mama's hand went to her mouth as she gasped. "I can't believe it. Todd…" She looked at me and then back at the coach and sank low in her chair. Disappointment and shock were written all over her face. She had believed my lies until then.

"I know this is bad, Mrs. Byrd, but…because he is so good at football, here's what we are going to do. We will send him to a 30-day outpatient drug rehab program. Then he can come on back just in time for the season to start. We want him to get to start as left defensive tackle." He pointed a finger at me and said, "Todd, you get the situation under control, and we're still going to let you play football."

Two days later, my mother had a stroke and was hospitalized for a few days. My older brothers accused me of causing the stroke.

One said, "You are driving our mama crazy."

Keith said, "He ain't done nothing you hadn't done already."

What they said bothered me real bad. I went every day after school to the drug program. They counselled me and asked questions. "Todd, why are you doing drugs? Are you depressed?" I told them whatever I thought they wanted to hear, and before long the 30 days were up, and I was back with the team.

Along the way, lying got easier, and I got real good at hiding stuff. I lied to my parents. I lied to my friends. I lied to everybody. I wanted people to like me and I cared what they thought. For example, I'd ask Mama to drop me off at the movie theater to meet my friends. After she drove off, I'd hook up with my buddies and go somewhere to smoke, drink, and do drugs. I always made sure to get back to the theater in time for her to pick me up.

"How was the movie, Todd?"

"It was great, Mama."

On the outside it looked like I had it together. I was active and playing sports. But, all along I was addicted to drugs.

Chapter 3
Being Tough

⌒

Mama stayed at home during the day, and Dad worked at the Veterans Hospital in Memphis 100 miles away. During the week, he stayed there with one of my brothers and came home on the weekends. Mom pretty much raised me, and she was strict as could be. Sometimes I pushed her to the max as a bad teenager. Up until around 15, I was afraid of her and showed respect. After that, drugs changed my attitude.

When I was a young kid in school, there was no pressure to do school work from the teachers. They emphasized my sports.

Some told me, "If you don't fight...if you don't cause a disturbance...you can just sit in the back of the room. Bring a *Hot Rod* or hunting magazine and just stay out of trouble. We're gonna pass you."

I made C+s and Bs all through school because of that. However, things changed when I failed the drug test. Then I was told, "You need to start doing your homework." Well, I had a problem with that. They did not realize that teachers had let me slide in junior high and then on to high school. Now, I *could not* do the work.

This embarrassed me, so I figured the best way to handle the situation was to lie. I told my parents, "They are treating me different now."

Mom said, "What do you want to do?"

"I'm going to quit."

"Aw, no. You're not quittin' school," she said.

I said, "How 'bout lettin' me go to Bradford High?"

I remember my dad looking straight at me and he said, "Boy, they don't even have a football team!"

"Dad, I ain't worried about football."

By this time, I was more worried about access to drugs than I was my opportunity to play sports. I transferred to Bradford. At the time what I thought was great, may have been the worst thing that could have happened to me.

At Milan High School, we had the Preps and the Hoods – a difference in two major groups. The Preps were typical, traditional students, and the Hoods acted like they were from the ghetto. But, when I got to Bradford, it seemed they were all Hoods. There were even cheerleaders doing drugs and drinking.

I thought, *Wow, this is it! This is where I need to be.* I finished my sophomore year and started my junior year.

I got into many altercations in school, either defending myself or defending others. I earned a reputation as a fighter. What other people thought, or who they said I ought to be, really controlled me. Now at 16, my reputation got me in a lot of fights. It didn't take much to light my anger fuse. In my junior year at Bradford High, I got into it with a dude at the pep rally over my girlfriend. I was high on methamphetamine. The guy, Bryan, bad-mouthed me. It accelerated. Angry words went back and forth.

The friends I sat with said, "Are you going to let him talk to you like that? We heard you was tough and we ain't seen it. We've just heard."

I said, "No. I'm not going to let him talk to me like that. When this pep rally is over, I am going to show you!"

After the pep rally, I met him outside. He was muscled-up, but shorter than me. He also had a big reputation for fighting in that school. We resumed our angry talk and needless to say, we got into it. We lunged at each other and started swinging. It erupted into a violent storm of punches and blows. The fight turned brutal, and in a rage, I pounded him. None of the teachers intervened because they were scared of me. One of my friends came around and grabbed me from behind my neck. I started to take a swing at him because I didn't know who had me.

He came in close to my ear and said in a hoarse whisper, "Byrd, if you don't stop, you're gonna kill him!" So I quit and backed up. They called an ambulance for that guy.

Mr. Patterson was the vice-principal at Bradford at the time and was in charge since Joe Denning, the principal, wasn't there that day. Mr. Patterson had no idea what to do. He'd never seen anything like that happen.

He said, "Do you have a change of clothes in your car?"

I was covered in blood. I said "Yeah." I'm thinking to myself, *They're not going to kick me out of school? They kicked me out of Milan for doing drugs. I thought surely they'd kick me out for this.*

He shrugged and said, "Change your shirt and come back to class. Brian left in an ambulance and here you are, so come on to class."

I thought, *I like Bradford. They're alright. I can't believe I got away with this.*

The next morning I pulled into the school parking lot in my blue '79 Toyota Corolla. Principal Joe Denning, stood on the porch with his arms crossed solidly over this chest. He'd never done that and I knew it was a bad sign. I got out of the car, and he started walking toward me.

He said, "Come here."

We met halfway across the parking lot.

He said, "Son, get back in your car and go home."

I said, "Just like that?"

"No, it isn't going to be just like that. Come back in two weeks and bring your parents. Here's the paperwork. You don't even need to sign it – just go."

I said, "Okay."

He put his hand on my shoulder and said, "As a person, you are a great guy. You got to leave the drugs alone. If you don't, you'll be in the state penitentiary."

I drove home, and Mama was upset when I showed up at the house. "Todd, why aren't you at school?" When I told her what happened, I saw the disappointment and worry on her face.

When Dad came home that weekend, I told him about the fight and that I was suspended for two weeks. In my defense, I said, "Dad, *he* started it."

He said, "Yeah, but you shouldn't have been in it — period!"

I said, "Yessir, I know."

Two weeks later, they carried me before the West Tennessee Special School District Board. I found out it took 22 stitches to close up Brian's forehead and he also had a broken nose and jaw.

After presenting their case, they officially kicked me out of the West Tennessee School system altogether. Our family would have to move to middle Tennessee or east Tennessee or another state for me to go to high school. My family did not have that kind of money, and that wasn't going to happen. So that day, I left out of there expelled from school in west Tennessee. My father sat me down and said, "Well, you gonna *act* grown, then you gonna *be* grown. If you live in this house, you're gonna have a job."

The following Monday I started work at the Kellwood factory in Greenfield, a city close to where I lived. The company boxed and shipped Levis, and I operated a forklift. Once I was working in an environment with grown people, I began selling drugs to support my habit and to make money. My addiction spiraled out of control. I moved out of the house.

Chapter 4
Happy Birthday

❧

I looked forward to my birthday every year. Mama always made a big deal out of it and baked a Red Velvet cake – my favorite. So, when I turned 18 years old, I drove up to the house early in the morning. I came in the back porch and into the kitchen. There on the bar between the kitchen and living room sat my cake, but Mama was crying.

Alarmed, I looked at Dad and said, "Is something wrong with Keith? Is he okay?" I thought maybe he had been drinking and had a car wreck or was in jail or something.

She said, "Your brother is fine...far as I know. We need to talk to you. Sit down."

Her eyes were red from crying. I knew this was bad. If my parents tell me to sit down, it ain't good. As I sank into the chair, I said, "What's goin' on?"

"We've got something to tell you," she said wiping her eyes. "We're not your parents. We're your *grandparents.*"

I couldn't believe what I was hearing. I blinked a few

times trying to absorb the words I just heard.

"Your brothers ain't your brothers. They're your uncles. The oldest one, Tom, was your father. He was our first son."

I stared in disbelief. Dad sat, not saying a word.

"The one you thought was your oldest brother and got buried alive – that was your dad. It was a construction accident. We ain't seen your mother since you was a baby…not since the day we adopted you. We don't know where she is."

Mama took a deep breath and said, "On top of this, here is $89,000." She handed me the check with a shaky hand. "There was a settlement of $30,000 from suing the state after he died. With interest, it is now this amount and because you are 18, it is yours. Happy Birthday."

Mama said, "Before you was born in 1973, your father did construction work. When your mother was a few months pregnant, he and the crew was working on a pipeline. On that Saturday, the foreman said, 'Here's what we can do. We can shore up this project, and it will take all day, and we'll have to work tomorrow. Or, we got just a few hours left, maybe two or three. We can choose *not* to shore it up, there's just a few feet left. We can knock this out.' They all agreed and got down there and got to work. The foundation caved in and buried your father alive with four other men."

"Wait a minute," I said. "All these years I heard stories about Tom and that he was the toughest one of my brothers. Now, you're telling me this was my *dad?*"

"Yes, Todd, and there's more to tell you. He rode for a well-known, tough motorcycle gang. Your mom was addicted to heroin and lived a rough lifestyle. After your father got killed, a few months later she gave birth to you. And a little later on, when you was probably two or three months old, she robbed a liquor store at gunpoint to help support her addiction. She got arrested. Then to cut a deal, she agreed to testify and turn State's Evidence against some of the bikers in the gang. Evidently, they had inside connections and they knew she was telling on some of the guys. Those folks take things like that serious. She was going to testify, and they caught wind of it and made a plan to stop her."

"Your mother and father lived together in a small apartment complex that was made up of four apartments. It was like a duplex with a duplex upstairs. She needed some cigarettes, so she picked you up and carried you out of the apartment. She was headed to a nearby house to bum a pack of smokes from her friend. No sooner than she walked out, KABOOM! An explosion rocked the neighborhood. That motorcycle gang had decided to kill her before she could testify and had strapped dynamite around the four-apartment complex and when it blew up, it leveled the entire building to the ground."

"In fear for her life, she took off upstate and got around some of your father's club members that didn't know about what was going on back home. She stayed there at the clubhouse. Then one day, she said to one of the guys, 'Hey, can you watch the baby for a few minutes? I need to make a run for some beer and cigarettes. I'll be right back.' He agreed to watch you. She walked out and never returned.

After a month's time they called us and said, 'Listen, we got this baby, Todd. This ain't no place for a baby. This is a clubhouse – no place for a child. Will you come and get him?' So we flew upstate and got you and brought you back. We filed for adoption. During the adoption process, your mother was in jail because she committed another armed robbery. She decided to fight the adoption, so we hired a lawyer. When it came before the judge, he ruled in our favor. He didn't sympathize with her at all. He said, 'You know you're saying that you want him now, but you *left* him at a drug house.' So, the adoption was finalized."

I fought back tears and anger. I said, "How could you lie to me all these years?" Then I thought about the money. Then I was shaken again by this news – my parents are not my parents. I tried to grasp it. "How did you let me believe it all this time?"

Mama said, "We saw that you was wild even from a baby. We used to put you in your baby pen and in a few minutes you was in the living room. So we actually hid to see what you did to get out of it. We peeked around and saw you pull yourself up with your fingertips, put your chin on the crib rail, squirm over it, and fall on the floor. You laid there for a minute 'cause it knocked the breath out of you. Then you shook it off and crawled into the living room. We knew you were going to be hard to handle. As time went by, we thought if we told you that we was your grandparents, you wouldn't listen to us and respect us."

Our talk lasted two, maybe three hours. I left without giving another thought to the cake. I felt betrayed. The ones I was closest to…they knew I wasn't their brother. My whole life was a lie.

I pushed away from all of them.

Chapter 5
Life in the Fast Lane

～∾～

Angry, confused, and suddenly rich at 18 years old, I intended to do right. I planned to straighten out my life and buy a house or some land with the money. My car choice was a red '91 Chevy Beretta GTU. Everyone could see me coming. I was now a "high-roller" with all that money, and people wanted to be my friend.

One day, I was in a hurry to get to a man's house in Bradford to pick up cocaine. I topped a hill doing 65 mph, hit water, and hydroplaned. I crossed over to the oncoming lane and hit a 1978 Ford work truck head-on. The car spun around and around. It broke my car in half and into an L-shape. My head knocked off the rearview mirror as I hit the windshield. I got a cut at the eyebrow. The three guys in the truck were okay, except the driver hurt his ribs on the gear shift. The State Trooper wrote it off as caused by hazardous weather. The damage to my car amounted to $9,000. After the repairs, I drove it for a while. Then I sold it and bought a cheaper vehicle to have more cash.

Then came the time while partying, I overdosed on LSD and drank the Dr. Pepper with pods in it. The police took me to the mental hospital and after 60 days I was released.

My time in the mental hospital didn't stop me. I picked up right where I left off. I still had lots of money. I got out, smoked crack, and partied. During that time, I had more friends than ever in my life. I was a real "giver" and wanted to help them out. If we were going to a party and somebody needed clothes, I bought them.

A teller at my bank always showed concern for me. I believe she was a friend of Mama. I didn't know anything about having a checking account, and I kept writing checks for more than was in my account. I took my mess in to get it covered by pulling money out of savings.

She had said, "Todd, what are you doing with your money? You need to slow down." She had known I was blowing a lot of money.

Then one day I pulled into the drive-in teller with my buddies in the truck.

I said, "I need to withdraw a thousand dollars."

She said, "You need to come inside."

I thought, *Here we go again. She is going to lecture me.* I parked and went inside.

She said, "There's no money in your checking account."

I pointed to the paper forms and said, "Let me fill out one of these. You take it out of savings and put it in checking."

She said, "No. Mr. Byrd, you don't understand. You are wiped out clean. You have no more money. As a matter of fact you owe us about $1,000 in overdraft fees."

I shook my head. I couldn't believe it. All my money was gone. I went out to my truck and told my friends, "Get out. The party's over! Get out. I'm broke."

It wasn't long before I sold the truck. Addicted to cocaine, I found myself homeless, living under a bridge for a while. People I had spent money on didn't want to be my friend anymore. I had bought cars, trailers, and land for people. When they saw me, walking 'cause I didn't have a vehicle anymore, they wouldn't even stop and give me a ride. Some let me stay with them a day or two, and then the same story came from each of them, "It ain't working out, you know. You're going to need to leave." Also, people knew the police were looking for me. It was a hard place for me.

There was a guy who owed me a large amount of money, around a thousand dollars. This came up in a discussion with my drug buddies. I ended up once again been influenced by what people thought of me.

They said, "You know you've got a reputation, and you can't let this guy get away with owing you money. What are you going to do about it?"

I said, "Carry me to his house while he is on lunch break. I'm either going to get my money or it's going to be a *bad* situation."

When we got to the small duplex where he lived, I saw him through the window moving around inside. I knocked. He wouldn't come to the door, so it made me mad. I kicked the door in and told him, "I want my money!" We hollered back and forth at each other, and then it escalated into a fight.

In the scuffle, I hit him in the head with a pistol and it cut him. He finally gave me a few hundred dollars. He owed me a lot more, but I said, "Okay. The debt is paid."

I got back in the car with my buddies. I knew down deep this wasn't the right thing to do, but I had done it.

A few weeks later, I called Mama just to check on her.

She said, "The Sheriff's Department was here looking for you. They had a warrant for your arrest."

I said, "What did the warrant say?" I had done so much illegal stuff then, I didn't know what they wanted me for.

She said, "Aggravated Assault and Aggravated Battery." The sound of her voice told me she was heartbroken.

I said, "I know what it's about." It was the guy who had owed me money. I had felt it was settled and the debt was paid.

I ran for a week, but they caught up with me. I went

to jail, posted bond, and got back out. I hung around my same so-called *friends*.

One of them said, "Man, that dude should have called it *even*. I can't believe he told on you."

Another guy said, "I know where he is staying now. He's with his cousin."

They kept ragging me about getting even.

All this fueled my anger, and I said, "Carry me there!"

Like a fool, high on drugs, when we got to the house, I kicked the door in. I whupped his cousin and then whupped him again for putting me in jail. I took a guitar and an amplifier and said, "*Now* we're even."

A few weeks later, when I called Mama she said, "The County was out here looking for you again. I thought you was out on bond."

I said, "Yes, ma'am, I am."

She said with a heavy voice, "They got another warrant with the exact same charges: Aggravated Battery and Aggravated Assault." I felt bad for her. I knew she was disappointed in me.

I kept on the run for a while. When I talked to Mama again, she said "Why don't you turn yourself in?" Her voice choked.

"Mama, I can't." I knew she didn't understand.

Then one day, I was at a loss of what to do. I had nowhere to go, and no place to live, and nothing to eat. I sat down on a bench next to the curbside stop for Greyhound. A police car pulled up to the stop sign in front of me. I walked over to the car, opened the back door, and proceeded to get in. It startled the cop, and he went for his gun. I held my hands up to show I meant no harm as I slid into the seat.

I said, "I'm tired and hungry and it is almost lunch time. Carry me to the County Jail."

He recognized me and knew I had an outstanding warrant. He said, "Close the door." He drove to the City Jail, where they fingerprinted me, and then transported me to County Jail.

When I went to court, they intended to reinstate my bond.

Dad stood up and said, "Your honor, can I say something?"

"Yes, sir. Who are you?"

"I am his father. The best thing you can do is keep him in jail until he gets over his drug addiction, because he leaves a path of destruction everywhere he goes. He's addicted to crack cocaine."

The judge looked at him and said, "I'm going to honor your wish." Then he looked straight at me, pointed his finger, and said, "Mr. Byrd, sit down. You are no longer a free man."

My case progressed to the Grand Jury, and now it was the State of Tennessee vs. Todd Byrd. My lawyer handed me a document. On it were listed the State's witnesses. I looked at him, pointed to the list, and said, "What does this mean? Why are my friends' names on this list? There are three of them on here."

He said, "Boy, that's the ones who are testifying against you."

I said, "Do what?" Those were the same guys steady telling me in the beginning, "Hey, are you going to let him get away with this?" Talk about feeling betrayed! I boiled inside.

Come to find out, they were on probation and had

been pulled over for running a stop sign. In the ashtray lay a roach clip (joint). To get a reduced sentence on their charge, they jumped at the chance to tell on me. The best place I could be that day was in jail, because if I found them it would've been a *bad* situation.

Chapter 6
Lake County Prison

❧

While still 18 years old in 1991, I went to Lake County prison. I had blown my only opportunity to make something of myself. I was ashamed and depressed over spending the money that came from my dad's death. In nine or ten months while trying to get high to stop thinking, I had blown all the money. I was in a fog.

In prison, I worked eight hours a day to get my GED. Time rocked on.

At the weight pile one day, there was a big muscled-up guy working out. He was *humongous*. I walked over near him and said, "Hey, can me and my crew get that weight bench next?" This guy, who looked like he'd been lifting weights 20 years, growled with foul language, "I'll tell you when I'm *done* with it."

I said, "O…kay."

As I walked away, the guys around me began to push me. It was a different crowd, but the same scenario playing out in my life. "Byrd, you gonna let that dude talk to you like that?"

I turned and faced them and said, "Did you see how *big* he is? I betcha he can talk to *you* like that!"

"No, when they talk to you like that in here, man, when you go to commissary, you may as well see what *he* wants every time. He'll control you. Don't let him talk to you like that!"

That night I couldn't sleep. I thought, *Man! What am I going to do? What in the world am I going to do?* I stayed up all night long debating with myself. I couldn't let it slide, him talking to me like that. *What will the guys think of me? Besides I can't let him be boss of me.*

Morning finally came. I carried a denim shirt with me and went to the yard. He was working out on the weight pile. I took a nickel (5 lb.) weight, and wrapped it up in the blue jean shirt. When he was on the incline bench press, I walked up behind him and swung the shirt, slamming him over the head with it. It split his head from his eye all the way back. I ran into my unit, into my cell, and some of my cellmates were there. I had blood all over me.

I said, "I done it. He ain't gonna bully me around anymore."

One guy hollered, "Get outta here!"

So I ran to the laundry and threw the stuff in the washing machine.

When the guards rushed in, they called me by number. "Inmate 2248, where is the weapon?"

I said, "I don't know what you're talking about. I been in here washing clothes."

"Get on the ground!"

They shoved me down, handcuffed me, and kicked me a few times.

A guard went to the first washing machine and pulled out the jean shirt with the weight still in it. Straight across it is read my prison number. He said sarcastically, "Are you *sure* you didn't assault nobody?"

Well, needless to say, I went to solitary – the hole. They pushed me in, and I looked around at the small, bare cell. It consisted of a concrete slab, a thin mattress, a toilet, and a shower. They locked me up away from the general population, and I would not be leaving that cell for any reason. I was scared. When the adrenaline rush was over, reality set in. I was afraid that Bates was going to die. That night around 6:00 PM, my counselor came to my cell, along with the chaplain.

The counselor said, "Todd, we need to talk."

I said, "Yessir." I'm thinking he's just going to read me off my charges.

He said, "We had to rush Inmate Bates… We had to helicopter him off this compound, and he is in ICU. It ain't lookin' like he's gonna live. I want to inform you, too, if he dies you will do the rest of your life in the penitentiary. You'll do the rest of your natural life."

The chaplain stood behind him. He stepped forward and said, "Son, would you like me to pray with you?"

I said "Naw. But, would you pray for him – that he makes it?"

He said, "Yes, sir." He bowed his head, and I watched him while he prayed. I hoped it would do some good. I thought to myself, *How did I get to right here?*

By the grace of God, Bates did not die.

Two weeks later, the prison held a disciplinary hearing to decide what they would do. They took away my "good time" and put me back in the hole. Because of the severity of what happened, they told me I was going to public court before the judge.

One week later, when they gave me an attorney, I went to court in a red jumpsuit, which indicates someone is a violent offender. The bailiff cleared the courtroom of everyone except me, my lawyer, and the judge. This was to prevent a security breach. I plead guilty.

Prior to this incident I had built up "good time" credit. That is the amount of time that will be reduced from the actual time an inmate has to be in prison. It is earned for good behavior and rewarded by the Bureau of Prisons (BOP) for following prison rules and staying out of trouble.

The judge took away my "good time," and gave me more years on my sentence. So a sentence I could have completed in nine months, eligible for parole, went to six years.

They carried me from a minimum security prison to a maximum security prison, Northwest. To transport me, my ankles were shackled together and wrists handcuffed, then all four limbs chained together at the waist, and then bolted to the floor of the van. (They don't bolt inmates to the floor anymore because a van caught on fire in Tennessee, and the inmates died.)

Chapter 7
The Hole

❧

I spent nine months in solitary – the hole. I had plenty of time to think. At times, I laid there and stared at the ceiling thinking back to where I lived growing up. From the time I was five years old, our home was on eleven acres of land that used to be a dairy farm out in the country. The property had a house with white vinyl siding, with concrete paths all around, a grain bin, concrete silo, and long pole barn. The old silage pond was dug out real deep and stocked with catfish and bream. We fed the fish with pellets and fished with cane poles.

My brothers were a good bit older so there weren't kids to play with out there in the country. I found ways to entertain myself. In that big wooden barn, carpenter bees drilled holes, and it was as if me and the bees played hide-and-seek as they went up to the hay loft and then came down again. They wouldn't sting, so after I tired of playing with them, I took a tomato stake and used it as a bat to knock 'em to the ground and then took them down to the pond and fed them to the fish.

One day, I took off and rode my bicycle straight through the old barn and onto the paved hallway. As I flew along, the bike chain came off and I couldn't stop. I sailed right into the pond, bike and all. Mama, busy picking strawberries in the garden, heard me holler. She ran to the pond and saw me struggling to keep my head above water. She couldn't swim, and neither could I. Mama snatched a cane pole, and reached it out for me to grab. She saved me! She pulled me out of the deep water, and then she cried and hugged me. Then she whupped me. Then she hugged me. Then she whupped me.

I said, "Mama stop! I'm okay!"

It scared her real bad. That summer when I was seven, she signed me up to take swimming lessons at the City park. She paid for me to learn how to swim.

I thought back to Dad raising his rabbit dogs — Beagles, I think. I remembered weekends he took us to the river with a camper on the back of his old 50s blue Chevy truck that had a white stripe.

I lay in my bed remembering how simple life was when I was a kid. We'd go visit Dad's brother, Uncle Ern. He lived in a little community and raised goats in a place called Blue Goose, TN. One day, I got out there in the shed while the big people were all inside talking and eating. I found an old football helmet and strapped it on. I got down with those goats at eye level and let the goats charge at me head-to-head.

Mama told Dad, "Go get him. He's letting the goats head-butt him!" Dad says to this day, the goats knocked the sense out of me.

There was a path through the field about 100 yards from my house that led to Great Aunt Mable and Uncle

Doss. I spent a lot of time with them. They were like grandparents to me. I smiled thinking of being in the swing with Aunt Mable. Uncle Doss made apple cider. I'd pick his apples and churn them and made the cider. He spent time with me because my dad was always gone. He paid me to catch turtles – two dollars each for all them I caught. He ate them.

My parents liked to watch *Hee Haw* on TV. I didn't understand the humor, and it made me hate country music. My favorite TV show was *The Incredible Hulk*. He was a tough guy, but had a big heart. He had to leave at the end of the story. He wasn't trying to do something wrong. It made me sad, and I wiped tears from my eyes every time.

My mouth watered as I thought of my favorite food. I remembered homemade pizza, fried green tomatoes, and Mama's homemade biscuits. The smell from the kitchen was so good. I tried to sneak her cookies, and that wooden spoon hit my hand. "Get outta here!"

I wondered how all those years I didn't know my parents were really my grandparents.

Growing up, my brother Keith told me, "You know you are not my brother. The gypsies came to town and left you. Look at yourself."

Hmmm. I was 6'3" and 300 pounds. Everyone else in the family was small. It did seem odd, but I didn't believe him. Me and Keith was always close. He was a bad influence on me, but he loved me. And he always took up for me.

I thought about a kid I played with growing up, Andy Farrow. His dad owned a glass shop. Andy killed himself over a girl when he was 18. He had just graduated from high school.

I remembered how trusting my parents were. They took me to town to the skating rink or the movie theater in Milan. When they dropped us off at the theater, we wouldn't go in. After they drove off, me and my friends would head to the alley behind the theater. There were abandoned buildings there or sometimes we walked down the railroad tracks and did our drugs. But when we went to the skating rink, good Christian people ran it and they wanted to see who dropped us off and who picked us up. It wasn't as easy to sneak off.

I thought about how much all my mess had hurt Mama.

***

Finally my nine months were up, and I got back with the general population. At Northwest Correctional, gang violence was common. It was nothing to see someone stabbed and killed once a week. When I walked to the chow hall, there was a concrete wall about nine feet tall that made a blind spot where the camera couldn't see. I don't know how many times I walked into that cut and saw a guy standing there in wait for somebody. I'd know something was up. The guy waiting there wore a jean jacket even, in the summer, and his hands were in his pockets. His head was covered with two toboggans that had been sewed together, with slits cut out for their eyes.

I'd wonder, *Is he fixin' to stab me?*

I'd walk by and the guy would say something like, "Hey, Byrd. We're fixin' to lock it down. You better get in there and eat fast."

I ended up spending four years in that prison. Finally my time for release came. When Dad came to pick me up, I was drunk on homemade prison wine. I got out in 1998 when I was 24 years old.

Chapter 8
On the Run

❦

I got a nice job working as a welder for A.O. Smith Automotive Products. The money was good, but once again drugs pulled me back. I was doing meth. Instead of letting my experience in prison rehabilitate me, I had a hard attitude. I'd been to the worse prison in the state, and it was nothing to me. I sold drugs on a new level because of hooking up with some guys and making more connections. I moved dope on a big scale.

Within two months, I violated my parole by failing the drug test. It must have been because the prisons were so full they gave me a couple of chances. The last time I failed the drug test, I told the lady I needed to get a check stub out of the car. I went out the door and just took off.

I moved to Memphis and worked as a bouncer at a strip club and sold drugs to the strippers. I got deeper and deeper in the stuff I was doing. Then there was an auto accident. A woman hit my vehicle, and her insurance company gave me a rental car while mine was being repaired. While I had the rental, I hit a bridge and totaled the car. I was afraid to report it because the police were after me for the parole violation, so I stayed on the run.

I got a call that Mama was in the hospital with a stroke. I traveled back and went to see her. She laid up there in the hospital bed and looked at me pleading with her eyes as she said, "Would you please turn yourself in?"

"Mama, why would you want me to go back to jail?"

She wiped a tear away and said, "At least in jail, I'd know where you are."

I loved Mama and felt bad for her. I was breaking her heart. Her expression said more than her words.

I walked out of the hospital that day, and the police sat in their car waiting on me. They had seen my motorcycle pull up. By then, I had been on the run for eight or nine months.

They read me my rights, then took me to the station and asked me questions.

"Mr. Byrd, Where is the stolen car?"

I said, "It is parked at Northgate Motel."

In a few minutes, I heard over the police radio, "Okay. We located the car. Ask him where the hood and the bumper is."

I said, "They're in motel room 17."

They radioed back that the motel manager had opened the door for them. Then I heard talking and then laughter like they had just solved a case. "We have recovered… the hood and bumper."

I got 18 months for violating probation, and they put the issue with the car on hold. They sentenced me to Lake County, the same minimum security prison where I 'bout killed that guy. I figured they just wanted to get rid of me and they'd let Bate's "home boys" do it for them.

My attitude was, "Go ahead and kill me. You're just putting me out of my misery."

After release from there, they charged me for the rental car I wrecked. They picked me up in Madison County, and I had to make bond. Grand theft auto was reduced to destruction of property, and I was sentenced to one year (365 days) house arrest and three years' probation. On the last day of my house arrest (the 364th day), I caught a new charge. They busted me selling drugs. A girl who turned informant showed up to do a deal wearing a wire.

Now I was charged with possession with intent to sell marijuana. They ran it all together and gave me a year jail credit for the house arrest. This time I was sentenced to Ft. Pillow State Prison, which is now W. Tennessee State Penitentiary.

I found myself in the County Jail waiting for transit to prison. (This could take three to four months.) I was right in the middle of washing dishes when I was told, "Byrd, there's someone here who wants to see you." I took my headphones off and stepped into the hallway. It was Chris Smith, an old friend I grew up with. The last time I saw him, he was messed up with crack and meth and was peeking out from his trailer.

I said, "Hey man!" I hugged him. I said, "I can hook you up. I got shampoo, deodorant, Walkman, radio… what did they get you for?"

He said, "I'm not in jail. I came by to see you." He told me about Jesus. I listened, but it went in one ear and out the other.

I said, "I'll look you up in a few years when I get out of Ft. Pillow Prison."

He said, "I'm going to be praying for you, Byrd."

Later on, I got caught selling drugs in jail, so they sped up my transport and sent me on to Ft. Pillow.

Chapter 9
God Calling

❧

I served my time there and when I came out continued with the drugs and meth. After a while, I asked an old friend named Crystal to come by and pick me up at the Dura Factory where I worked because I needed a ride. We drove along and talked.

She said, "There's a revival going on. Will you go to church with me on Friday night? Chris Smith is going to be speaking."

"Are you crazy? The roof will fall in if I walk in there! Naw, I'm good. I'm not gonna be a hypocrite. I'm not gonna smoke dope and drink on Saturday night, and go to church on Sunday."

She just let me talk. I saw such a change in Crystal. A few years back she still partied with alcohol and drugs. She was a dependable friend, always there for me if I needed anything. Something dramatic had happened to her and I found out about it that afternoon when I got into the car with her. Christian music played on the radio.

She said, "Jesus loves you, Todd."

I said, "Why are you driving your grandma's station

wagon?"

"One night, I was drinking and took some pills, and passed out behind the wheel. The car ran up an embankment, flew between two trees, slid sideways, and stopped at the steps going up into a church. The way it landed, I could have opened the passenger door and walked into the foyer. I was still passed out when the pastor came out to see what had caused all the noise. He woke me up and got me into the church. He told me God had better plans for me, and after talking to me for a while, I gave my life to the Lord."

Now here we were years later, and she invited me to church. She brought her son over, and I took him down to the playground for a while. My girlfriend and I decided to go with her to church.

We slipped in and sat on the back row of the First Assembly of God in Milan, TN. My previous church experience took place years ago as a kid. Mama made me go to the Baptist church down the street. Now, I felt awkward and out of place. In my mind I wrestled with thoughts that people wondered what in the world *I* was doing there. I had such a reputation of being hard and tough.

People got to worshipping God and jumpin'. I had one foot in the aisle and eyes looking toward the door.

I leaned over and said, "Crystal, what's goin' on? What's wrong with her?" I nodded toward a lady dancing and shouting, hands up. Another lady started laughing and laughing — I wondered if it was evil. Nothing was funny. Why was she laughing?

Crystal said of the dancing lady, "She's full of the Spirit."

That didn't quiet my fears. After the singing, the place calmed down. Chris Smith preached a sermon and I just *knew* he was talking straight to me. Then, after a while, he gave an altar call asking people to come down if they wanted to ask Jesus into their life. I had no intention of doing anything – just ready to go home. But something happened, I'll never forget. A woman sitting in front of me turned around during the altar call and said, "Todd, if you died right now, would you go to heaven or…or would you go to hell?"

I was surprised when she called me by name. I didn't know how she knew it. I intended to lie to her and say, "I would go to heaven." I opened my mouth and could not speak. Nothing would come out. It was like my mouth was muzzled, so I kind of shook my head and shrugged and put my hands up like, "I don't know."

She said, "Don't you think you need to walk down that aisle?"

Somehow, I got up and started walking that way. Chris came down from the platform, coming toward me, and grabbed me with a hug. He whispered in my ear, "I extended this altar call for five minutes. I thought I was going to come *get* you!"

After that, I started going to church attended services every Sunday and Wednesday. One day, I came in from work and found a letter from the girl I lived with.

It said, "Pack up all your stuff and leave. You're trying to live your life for God. I'm not ready. We're on two different levels. I don't understand how we can go from doing all of this, and all of a sudden, like flipping on a light, you are following God. I'm not ready."

The alternator had gone out on my Ford Ranger, so I

called Chris to come pick me up. I said, "Brother, can I come sleep on your couch for a little while till I can find me a place?"

He said, "Absolutely. I'm on my way."

I packed up a few clothes and in the meantime, my girlfriend came home and she had been drinking. I told her that I was leaving, and Chris was coming to get me. She sat down and stared off into space, waiting. In a short time, Chris showed up, and I walked out to meet him with my stuff.

He said, "You go on out and wait in the van. I want to go inside and pray for her."

I sat in the van, and the devil started working on me. Thoughts bombarded me: "What kind of man are you? She needs help, too. You can't run out on her. You are abandoning her." My mind switched directions. Chris came out and cranked up the van. By the time we got to the stop sign, I said, "Hey man, I'm getting out." I reached for the door handle.

Chris said, "What are you doing?"

"I can't leave her. I'm going to work on her. Everything is gonna be okay."

Chris said, "Let me tell you something. You are new in Christ. You've got to focus on *you*. You are too immature right now in your walk. She's going to end up dragging you down."

"Chris, I got this. I've got big shoulders, I got this." He drove me back to my place, and I took my stuff out of the van and went back inside.

After a few months of me not showing back up for church, I heard a knock on the door. It was Chris. I've always been big on looking people in the eye when I talk to them, but this time couldn't do it.

He said, "What's going on?"

I said, "Life."

"You said it in those few words. You're back on drugs, right?"

"Yeah," I said, as I looked up at him. "Chris, in the beginning with church, I felt something I've never felt before. It was a great feeling coming to the Lord. But you gave me a Bible, and it was filled with *thou* and *hath*, and I can barely read. I can't understand it." I swept my hand around the room and said, "I understand this other world that I've been living in."

Chris said, "After coming to know God and going back to the ways of the world, it's seven-fold. Do you understand?"

"No, what do you mean?"

"Well, everything you've been through in your life, it's gonna be seven times worse. In the Book of Matthew it tells about it. I don't think you can make it."

I remember watching him drive away and thinking, "Man, that's pretty deep." His words kept going over and over in my head. "Seven-fold, seven times worse."

Chapter 10
Seven-Fold

ooking back, I could sure see that Chris was right. A few months prior to his visit, I had stopped going to church and slid back full-blown into the drug scene. I was the area drug dealer.

One bad thing that happened was one night I got meth on my finger and yawned, rubbing my eyes. The meth on my finger set the left eye on fire with pain! We took off to the closest hospital. The doctor tried different things to neutralize whatever I got in my eye. Finally I told them the truth about the dope. The meth burned a hole through my cornea leaving me partially blinded.

Another thing happened. One night at midnight, while high on meth, I was dropped off at a friend's mobile home out in the country and gave her some dope. A guy came by and wanted some drugs.

He recognized me. "Are you Todd Byrd? Do you know who lives next door?" He proceeded to tell me that a guy I'd had trouble with lived there. I went ahead and sold some drugs to him, and he left.

A couple of hours later, he showed up with that neighbor and three of his buddies. I had gone to school with these boys, and they knew I had drugs they could steal and that I didn't have a gun. They stood outside the trailer, and I heard them yelling for me to come out. "Byrd, come on out here!"

"Hey, Byrd let's see how tough you are!"

I looked out the window, saw them, and turned to my friend. "Take your kids to your grandma's and don't come back. There's going to be trouble."

She got the kids and left. I walked outside and pointed at the one I had an issue with. "This is just between me and Jimmy."

The two other guys backed off, and we charged at each other swinging. I whupped him and had him in a strong grip around the neck. They decided to gang up on me.

As I saw this, I said, "Back off, or I'll snap his neck."

They charged me grabbing anything they could get their hands on. They grabbed crutches and a bat off the wooden porch and started swinging and clobbering me. It turned into a full-fledged battle and made its way into the trailer. By then, someone grabbed a frying pan and hit me on the top of the head with it again and again. They used what was in their hands and beat me.

The frying pan was the worst. Every time the guy hit me on the head, my sight went black, and I was temporarily blinded. Eventually one of the guys grabbed a butcher knife and stabbed me several times. The guy with a pistol shot at me. The beating lasted several hours. It got brighter as daylight approached, and we knew the school bus came then.

Somebody yelled, "Let's get out of here before someone calls the cops!"

I hollered, "I'm not going anywhere until somebody gives me my flip-flops!" I didn't want to walk on gravel barefoot. They took off.

In a state of shock, I walked down the road, scared. I knew I was hurt bad. Parts of my body were numb. I kept feeling the top of my head to see if my skull was cracked open. The touch felt wet. I knew it was blood. My good eye swelled shut and I could barely see. I found a house and banged on the door.

A man opened it, and when he saw me, said, "Son, have you been in a car wreck?"

"Naw, it wasn't a car wreck. Can I use the phone and have a glass of water?"

"Sure." He came back with a cordless phone wrapped in a hand towel to protect it from the blood. I called my dad while the man went to get me a glass of water. Blood ran into it as I gulped it down.

"Sir, I'm sorry about getting blood on your carport and this glass."

He shook his head.

Dad arrived and stormed up to the house. "Who did this to you?" I told him who the guys were. He fumed. I knew he had a license to carry a handgun and was afraid he would do something. He stopped to use the payphone at a store and called the police. They came to the store, and Dad gave them the names of the boys and where they lived.

Dad sped down the road to the hospital in Milan. When they saw my condition, they rushed me to the trauma unit at Jackson-Madison Co. General Hospital, 34 minutes away in Jackson.

After checking me over and treating my stab wounds and other injuries, I was placed in the Intensive Care Unit. The big concern was the possibility of swelling of the brain. Tubes and wires went everywhere as they monitored me closely. I could barely see. My good eye was swollen shut.

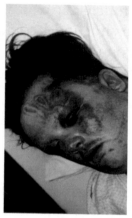

At one point in ICU, the doctor came in and asked the nurses to step out for a minute. When they left, he leaned in close and said to me. "Son, do you believe in God?"

I said, "Yeah. I believe there's a God."

"Get close to Him. Son, I've seen people who were literally beat to death and you look worse than they did. You don't have a broken or fractured bone in your body. God had to be with you. You need to get close to Him, do you understand me? Then he said, "Do you mind if I pray for you?"

I said, "Okay."

He prayed and then he looked me straight in the eye and said, "What are you going to do from here?"

I said, "I'm fixin' to find them boys and kill 'em."

***

The police arrested one of the boys the night of the fight, and he turned State's Evidence to get off light. All the other boys went to prison over this. An investigator came to my hospital room and tried to get me to testify, but I wouldn't do it.

When I got out of the hospital, me and a buddy went looking for them. When we saw the car, we flashed our lights. The guy pulled over and sped off. He ran a lady's car off the road into the ditch and got away because we stopped to help her.

Another time, I saw one of those guys, and when he saw me, he pulled into a church parking lot, of all places. I let it go. I never saw the others until I went back to prison.

Chapter 11
Despair

❧

At the end of 2000, my lifestyle was really getting to me. On the outside it looked great. Even though I had accumulated $60,000 in cash, prepaid the lease on my house for the next six months, had friends, and everything I wanted, I was miserable. I was deep in my addiction and my habit cost $1,000 day. I tried to stop cooking meth, but kept it up to support my habit or I'd burn through my cash.

In my mind I tried to figure it out. *I can't get off the dope. These are not really my friends. They are just here for what they can get from me. I'm either going to die of an overdose or go to prison. It is just hopeless.*

I drove my truck out to the farmhouse where I had lived all my life. It sat empty now because Dad had moved out. I walked up to the barn and then on to the edge of the pond where I sat down on a timber.

Tears streamed down my face. *I'm going to end it all. All this money…people don't really care about me…it is just my money. I know eventually I'll be back in prison.* I cocked my gun and chambered a bullet, raised my 9 mm pistol and put it to my temple.

"Todd." Someone called my name.

Was that God?

"Todd." I heard it the second time. I quickly brought down the gun from my head. The voice was from a friend I had grown up with and known all my life. She didn't see the gun.

"What are you doing?

"Just sitting out here by myself."

"You been crying?"

"No. I'm tired. Sitting here thinking. I've been in and out of prison my whole life. People are around me just for what they can get."

She felt my pain and had some of her own and we cried together for a moment. She tried to encourage me and then said, "You got any dope?"

I realized then she had seen my truck and pulled in because she was looking for drugs. Even though she was there for only one reason, she kept me from ending my life.

Chapter 12
Mama

❧

I did it again – violated parole. This time as a felon possessing a firearm. When I went before the judge, he said, "If it was up to me, You'd do the rest of your life in prison." I was one point away from being put away for life. He gave me 86 months (a little less than nine years).

I was being sent to Federal Correction Institution, a medium-high security prison in Memphis.

In the meantime, I was in "classification," where a prisoner is held until being sent to a prison based on their conviction. The process could take a couple of months.

While there, I got the message, "Your mom is hospitalized. She's in bad shape and will probably die." She had been diabetic, and none of us knew it. Later the family found syringes, and discovered she had never taken her insulin. When I got the message about her, she had already had surgery.

They shackled me hand and foot and carried me to see her. Two women prison guards escorted me to the hospital. They took the shackles off my wrists. One said,

"I know you can't run fast with those shackles on your ankles, but if you try to, we'll shoot you." She smiled, but I knew she meant it.

Dad met me outside the room and said, "They have amputated her leg above the knee." My heart sank. I fought back tears.

When Mama had been sick before, she said, "I wouldn't want to live if something happens and people have to take care of me."

I took a deep breath. I wanted to be strong, so I put up a front. Dad and I walked in together. I looked around the room and saw a couple of my brothers slouched in chairs. The doctor stood by the foot of the bed. There she lay, hooked up to machines. Mama woke up for about five minutes while I was there. She smiled at me. I took her hand. Then she cried when she recognized the denim prison uniform. It had a white stripe with my inmate number on it. When I saw her tears, I busted out crying, too. Because of all the things she was hooked up to, I could not hug her. After she dozed back off, I talked to the doctor.

"She's getting stronger," he said.

"Doc, tell me straight. Don't just *tell* me she's getting better," I said.

"I'm telling you the truth," he said.

The next day, she passed away – a stroke caused by a blood clot from the surgery. I was 28 years old. It hurt so bad that she died. I wanted to smash the doctor! I felt like he lied to me.

Plans were made for a service, and I got permission to go to the funeral home. Again, I was shackled wrists and feet. The police said my whole family had to clear out of the place before I could go in.

My dad spoke up and said, "I ain't leaving. I raised him and I'm staying in here with him." He stayed.

Guards watched the back of the building to be sure I didn't pull anything. All my family wanted to hug me. I was afraid at first they were causing trouble with the guards. I was there for 15 minutes, and they wouldn't let me go to the graveside.

This tore me up inside. When I got back to the prison, I didn't want anyone see me break down. I walked by myself on the bridge-way back to my unit. A black female guard saw me and the look on my face. She reached out and put her arms around me and held me. I cried like a baby. She offered me a cigarette and told the guards to let me out if I needed to use the phone. I'll never forget her.

Chapter 13
Hefe

❦

I arrived at the prison in Memphis. It didn't take long to get the feel of the place. It was tough. They put me to work on a plumbing crew.

On one of my stints in prison, I had worked on a construction crew and got my Maintenance Degree. We had done the book training and then had done projects. We had built a shuffle board and a pavilion.

In this prison, there were 148 cells on two floors. Two-man cells made up the top floor. The bottom floor consists of three-man cells with concrete block walls separating us for privacy and quieting the noise between us. I was in a three-man cell.

One day the guy in the cell next to me said, "You, *hefe.*"

I said "Hefty? I don't appreciate you calling me *fat.*"

He said, "No. *Hefe* means "boss" in Spanish. Whether you know it or not, you are the boss of the white people in here."

In a short time, it turned out to be true. My image of a tough guy got around, and I became the leader of a

250-member prison gang. In the B.O.P. (Bureau of Prisons), there are a variety of gangs, like fraternities. Not all the prisoners join a gang, but the benefits include protection and control of prison rackets like drugs, alcohol, power, and respect. The inmates soon learn it is better to be feared than loved. Many join for the protection afforded by the gang.

When I first got in prison, my tattoos were crude. Then when I got to Federal prison I had a cellmate who had been a professional tattoo artist on the street. He fixed up the tats that weren't so good and tied them altogether in sleeves covering both arms. The guards did not allow it, so we waited at night on their patrols. Every two hours they came by, so the artist would work until 20 minutes before he was due to come by.

Age 31 in prison

I've got a tattoo on my arm that is a picture of the devil praying. When Terry, my cellmate, was tattooing the full sleeve on my right arm, there was an empty space left on the inside of the upper part. I asked him, "What are you going to tattoo there? Why don't you draw up something that makes you think of me."

He said, "Okay, Byrd."

He started sketching out the devil praying.

I said, "What in the world is that for?"

He said, "Byrd you are so mean, I think the devil prays for mercy."

I said, "That's cool. Put it on there," as I pointed to empty space on my arm.

It was a hard crowd in there, full of drama day after day. There was never any peace. Things were always on edge and kept me wondering what was going to happen next. We had lots of stuff going on. I got into an altercation with another gang out on the yard, and they sent me to the hole for fighting. The procedure is, if someone is sent to the hole, the guard locks their cell and then someone goes to pack up his personal stuff.

When the guard working my unit was ready, he asked my cellmate, "Which locker is Byrd's?"

The guy told him, and he packed up my stuff. Then he smelled the hidden wine brewing in the vent over the sink and confiscated it. This meant I was in even more trouble.

Prison wine called for creativity. All you needed was a little knowledge, something that would ferment, and time. We used all forms of fruit, including oranges and fruit cocktail, and added sugar, water, and other ingredients to make something intoxicating. It fermented and smelled horrible, but drinking it made you high.

I was to have a disciplinary hearing and be officially assigned to the hole 30 days for fighting.

Chapter 14
A Squeaky Wheel

❧

The second week in the hole, I heard a familiar sound coming down the corridor. I knew it was the chaplain because of the cart he pushed with a wobbly wheel. As it got closer, he said, in a voice sounding like Count Dracula from Transylvania, "Would… you… like… something…to read?"

"Naw!" I said, as I kicked the door. I got back on my bunk, and then he slid something under my door. I went to the door and said, "Hey!" I heard the cart wobble on off with its squeaky wheel. I picked up what he had put under the door, and saw it was a 365-day devotional.

I had nothing to do, so I started reading. I read the book cover to cover in two days. I thought about my life and the mess it turned out to be, and when I finished, I fell on my knees. *God, I'm tired. I'm broken. I'm through living life the way I've been living. I want to know You. I want a relationship with You.* I looked around the cell. *God, this ain't me. This ain't who I am.*

I made a decision that day to follow Jesus. I surrendered and gave God my life. A peace came into my cell that I cannot describe. I said, *God if You let me out of this hole, I'm leaving the gang.*

Three days later, they came to get me as a witness for the hearing of someone else's case. In the prison, I worked in construction maintenance as head of plumbing. A guy in my crew had thrown a bolt at an officer.

"Byrd, did you see Inmate Hobbs throw a bolt at the officer?"

I lied, "No, sir. I did not see him throw it. When told to, he gently put it in the cart."

"Inmate Hobbs just admitted that he threw it, and you just lied. You'll get more time in the hole for lying! And stay right here. You're up next for your *own* disciplinary hearing."

The Disciplinary Hearing Officer addressed my case and read the charge of fighting. The Investigating Officer said, "We have additional charges. We found wine in his cell."

They had the evidence. "Is this your wine?"

I said, "Yessir."

"Do you plead guilty?"

"Yessir."

He found me guilty and told me his decision, "Thirty days for fighting and 30 more in the hole for making wine."

They sent me out to wait in the hall with the other prisoners having hearings. Guards stood watch over us.

A lieutenant came by and asked me what happened. I told him I'd be in the hole for 60 days. He went into the meeting room, and I heard arguing back and forth. After a few minutes, he came out to get me and said, "Come in and *don't* say a word."

The Disciplinary Hearing Officer said, "In construction maintenance you are the head plumber, and I'm told they need you. I'm putting the 60 days on the shelf. If you as much as spit on the sidewalk, it will turn into 120 days. Your record shows you will be right back in trouble."

They took me back to the hole. I got my stuff and carried my property bag back in the room to my original cell and threw it on the bunk. Here came my old "knuckleheads."

One guy said, "We know who told on you, Byrd. We're gonna smash him."

He wouldn't believe no one told on me. So I looked at him hard and decided to follow his train of thought. "Have you ever stopped and thought about it? If a person is so lost from God that he would tell on me, knowing what I would do to him, how 'bout praying for him?"

He looked at me and said, "Man, what's wrong with you?"

"Ain't nothing wrong with me. Everything is starting to fix itself out. I just accepted Christ as my savior in the hole, and I'm going to live my life for Him. Now if y'all want to beat me – I know (in gangs) it is beat in and beat out… Get to beatin'. Whatever the outcome is, I'm done. Y'all find a new leader. It ain't me no more. I ain't in the gang no more. I'm following God."

The guys kinda looked at me crazy and walked away. I think they were waiting for me to come to my senses.

A gang is brotherhood. It was hard to walk away from it. I had led them and now told them they were on their own. However, people started coming to me and asked me for advice. "What do you think we ought to do about this?"

I would tell them, "Hey man, have you thought about praying about it? How about turning it over to God?"

As time went by, they stopped asking me for wisdom. During the nearly four years I remained in prison, a guy who came to preach on Sundays also came and taught me the Bible two nights a week. It strengthened me, and I'd like to thank him one day.

Chapter 15
Getting Serious with God

∽

After release from prison, I got a job as a welder. I drifted back into drinking. I met Dee, the woman I am married to now.

Years prior to this, I had been in a relationship with a girl named Julie, and we had a son named Daniel. I hadn't seen them in years. She came down from Cleveland to visit her family for Christmas and got in touch with me. Daniel was now 16 years old. We spent time together, and I bought him some Christmas presents.

Julie said, "Can we talk away from your girlfriend?"

I said, "Sure." So we got off somewhere to talk.

She said, "First of all, Todd, I want to tell you that I love you and want to be with you. I want us to raise our son together."

I looked her in the eye and said, "Julie, there is a difference in loving you and being in love. I will always love you because you are the mother of my child, but I don't love you no more."

She said, "Well, if you don't love me, there's nothing for me here. I'm going back to Cleveland and taking Daniel with me."

She went back to Cleveland, and four days later I got a phone call from her sister. She said, "Todd, are you sittin' down?"

"Yeah, what's going on?"

"Julie took a bottle of sleeping pills last night and killed herself." I collapsed into a chair, stunned at the news. The shock settled down over me. I hung up the phone.

Right then I said, "Dee, listen. There ain't going to be no more playing church. We need to find a church and get close to God, or I'm going to end up in the penitentiary and they won't *ever* let me out. Before I went to prison the last time, the federal judge told me, 'You've lived a life of crime. You've missed the Career Offender Act by one point. If you get so much as a speeding ticket, you will be in federal prison. I'm following the guidelines and giving you nine years, but if it was up to me, you'd spend the rest of your life behind bars.'"

She said, "Well, I'm not coming to visit you in prison."

We went on a journey visiting churches.

Eventually we came to the Vineyard Church in Milan, TN. I sat there that day looking around, trying to get a feel for the place, and rubbed my neck. It had stiffened up and got in a bind. This was the result of many injuries: a broken collar bone, a car wreck, fights I had been in, and prison guards who had hurt me. It had gotten to the point that when I turned my head to look at something, I had to turn my body. We sat there and I said to Dee, "When I get paid again, I need to go to the chiropractor."

The church had a time of praise and worship. Larry Eddings walked up to the pulpit and said, "Today we're going to do something a little different. I feel the Holy Spirit moving. Anybody that needs healing or prayer, come forward."

I looked at Dee and said, "Hey that's me – my neck." We both went to the altar, but to different areas.

When Larry got to me, he pulled out his anointing oil and said, "There is no power in this oil, but it represents the Holy Spirit, and there is power in God. I'm going to put it on my hand and lay my hand on your forehead." He did that and prayed for me and then stopped. I was waiting for him to say, "Amen." Then I saw him looking up and talking to God, but not out loud. He looked at me and said, "I'm fixin' to lay my hand on your neck." He said, "God, you know what he came for." He laid his hand on my neck and then a few moments later, I turned to walk away. I took two steps, and then turned my head to the left and then to the right, and it was healed!

When I got back to my seat, I looked up and Dee was walking toward me.

She said, "Have you been talking to that guy?"

I said, "No, ma'am."

"Well, he just told me everything that was holding me back from serving God – all the hold-ups that have kept me from coming to the Lord!"

I said, "Dee, if you think that's something – look at me!" I turned my head left and right. I was convinced that God was there, and I wanted it all.

After we left the church that day, I said to Dee, "We can't go to church and live in sin. We can't just *live* together. I will move out, or we will get married." We got married May 3, 2014.

My life was still kind of a roller coaster ride. I was hot and cold when it came to doing everything I should be doing. I was sitting in a deer stand one day and texted Larry my testimony. He called me and said, "We need to meet. I've been praying for a true disciple, and I believe it's you."

I told him then, "I've been on a roller coaster ride."

He took the time to disciple me. A disciple is a disciplined one. I needed someone to mentor me and a person I could be accountable to for my choices and behavior. It was great to know someone was committed to me and prayed for me. That was three years ago. Now, I am an ordained pastor of the Vineyard Church in Milan, TN.

Chapter 16
The Next Step

∾

I f you relate to my story and know you are on a path of destruction, instead of digging your hole deeper, take time right now to consider your choices. Continue down the same path, or choose a new life.

If you are in prison, I know it is not an easy path in there, but you have to get to the point that you realize it is not working, and recognize there has be to a change in your life. Satan wants us to take the road to destruction. It gets harder. Put your faith in God. Let Him work out all your problems.

I want this book to impact you. I want you to know there is a better way! You can overcome. You can do all things through Christ who strengthens you. You can never go so far, that you're out of the reach of Jesus.

John 16:33 Take peace in me and know that in this world there will be tribulation …

All things are possible with God. The eternal resting place is what matters. I love you, and Jesus loves you.

Decision time. Every time I was arrested, I had to put my hands in the air to surrender. I'm inviting you to do this.

Here is an opportunity for you to surrender right now, to the Lord. If you do that and fully follow Him, you don't have to go down those dark paths that I went down. We've got a good God, and He loves us.

Having read this book puts you in a position for breakthrough. If you have never asked Jesus into your life and accepted what He did for you, now is a good time to do it. If you prayed for salvation at some point in your life, but have drifted away from God, you can be restored to a right relationship with Him.

In order to be saved, born-again, we must confess with our mouth and believe in our heart.

Do you believe that Jesus died for the sins of the world (that includes you)?

Do you believe Jesus was raised from the dead?

If so, pray this prayer:

God, I thank You for giving me the faith to make a commitment to You.

I choose to receive what Jesus did on the cross for my salvation.

Jesus, come into my heart.

Forgive me.

Save me and set me free from: (name what you want to be free from _____).

Lord, lead me in choices I need to make.

I receive Your grace which will empower me to live above sin.

Afterword

◆

My first recollection of Todd Byrd was when we were both pretty young; my best guess is about ten to twelve years old. We both attended Oakwood Baptist, a small country church just outside the city limits of Milan, TN. Todd always gave the preacher a hard time and was a cut-up whenever we were at church functions, but was never a troublemaker. Our paths took different directions as we got into high school. Todd hung out with a different group of kids than me and I noticed changes in him, not just in his appearance, but in his actions. I had never been exposed to drugs prior to high school, and as I started hearing about kids experimenting with marijuana, I was kind of shocked and surprised. I was a couple years ahead of Todd in high school, so after I graduated our lives went separate ways and I didn't see him much for a few years.

In 1994, when I was 24 years old, I got into law enforcement in a nearby town. In 1995, Milan Police Dept. hired me, and I was back working as a police officer in the town we grew up in. It didn't take long after that for my path to start crossing Todd's path. I heard he had been in and out of jail a few times, mainly for drugs. Once I started seeing him running with a certain group of individuals, I knew he was in deeper than I ever imagined a kid I grew up with would be. He had heard the same preaching I heard, and I couldn't believe the path he was going down.

Fast forward until probably 2001, and methamphetamine started to be a real problem in our area. It was new to us in rural West TN, although other parts of the country had been dealing with it for some time. I heard from our narcotics investigators that Todd was running in the circle of people they believed were starting to cook meth and distribute it in our town. I saw more and more of Todd around town, and usually with people he shouldn't be associated with.

December, 2001, on a cold day, I was on patrol for the city of Milan on day shift. I pulled out of Milan High School parking lot and noticed a red pickup truck coming into town that looked like the truck I'd seen Todd and his girlfriend driving. I decided to wait and let it pass me to see who was driving it. Sure enough, as it went by, I saw Todd in the passenger seat and his girlfriend driving. Neither even so much as glanced in my direction as they drove by, which is usually an indicator that something isn't right. It's that thing – if I don't look at them, maybe they won't look at me! I followed the truck into town and pulled them over for a traffic violation. As I got out of my patrol car and walked up to the driver side, I glanced over in the back of the truck and noticed a backpack laying there. I eventually recovered in it all the paraphernalia for a meth lab, and Todd had a bag of meth in his cigarette pack that he had actually just cooked prior to me stopping them. That was the last time I had any contact with Todd for several years. He eventually went to Federal prison, and I heard he got a 10-year sentence.

I tell that story now, almost with some sense of pride, but not because I put Todd in prison. I like to think the events that unfolded in his life after that, his intervention by our Lord and Savior, never would have happened if Todd had not found his rock bottom. He realized the only way to come up from it was to pray and acknowledge that an innocent Man's blood was shed to wipe away all the wrongs we had done. I listen to Todd's testimony now, and my eyes tear up every time I hear it, knowing where he came from and seeing where he is today. I never see Todd that he don't grab me up and give me a big hug. Typically he follows up that the next day with a text telling me how good it was to see me and that he loves me. I'm blessed to call Todd Byrd my friend and brother in Christ today!

Sheriff Paul Thomas
Sheriff of Gibson County, Trenton, TN.

Sheriff Thomas and Todd Byrd

About the Author

❧

Todd Byrd serves as lead pastor of Milan Vineyard Church. He is the county coordinator for Teen Challenge and serves on the Drug Court Panel of Gibson County. He and his wife, Dee, reside in Milan, TN.

About the Writer

❧

Sherry Anderson is a teacher, writer, and prayer leader. She is an adjunct professor at Gulf Coast State College, teaching the craft of writing. Sherry has published two nonfiction books, *Rising From Defeat: The Overcomer's Handbook* and *My Memory Serves Me Well*, the memoir of a Holocaust survivor.

Sherry has been a leader in Aglow International for many years. She is president of Writers Aglow in Panama City, where she has trained and coached writers for the past nine years. Writersaglow.com